WALRUS SONG

Janet Lawler

illustrated by

Timothy Basil Ering

CANDLEWICK PRESS

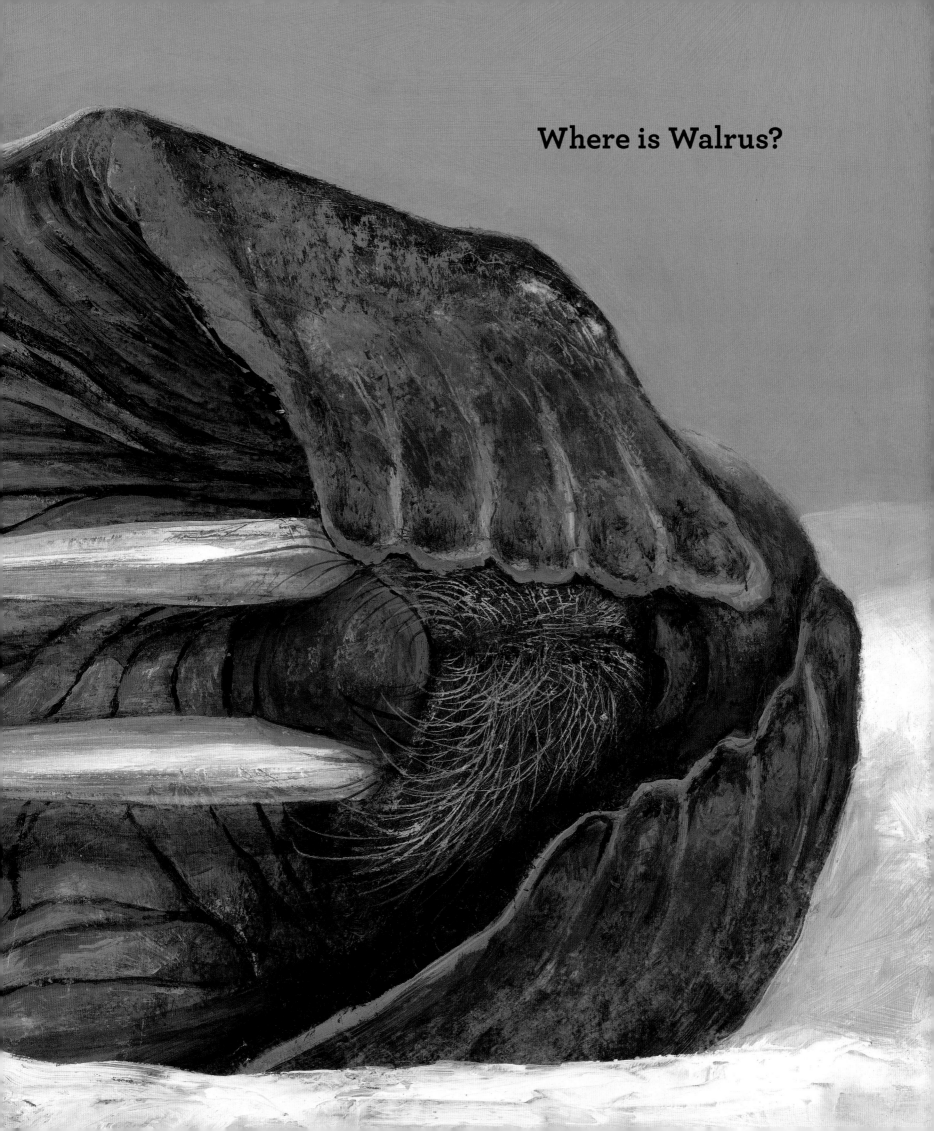

Where is Walrus?

On a floe.

He flops.

He plops!

Where did he go?

Twirling, whirling,
flippers swirling,

warm within his fat-lined coat,
solid, massive like a boat.

In icy waters,
Walrus dives,
seeking spots
where bivalves thrive.

Digging, wiggling,
whiskers jiggling,

Walrus, sea beast,
wants a clam feast.

What's he doing?
Seafloor stewing.

Lips on shells, Walrus sucks,
slurping clams, leaving shucks.

Belly full.
Time to play!
Sneak beneath—

surprise!

Gleaming tusks,
long and stout,

Walrus, hauling,
up and out.

Waddle. Walk.

Slap! Slap!

Walrus lumbers.

Flippers flap.

Now where's Walrus?
There's his muzzle!
Hundreds, thousands
nudge and nuzzle.

Walrus fight,
blubbered might,
clashing, crashing,
tusks a-bashing.

What's the ruckus?
What's that sound?

Walrus calls and songs
astound—

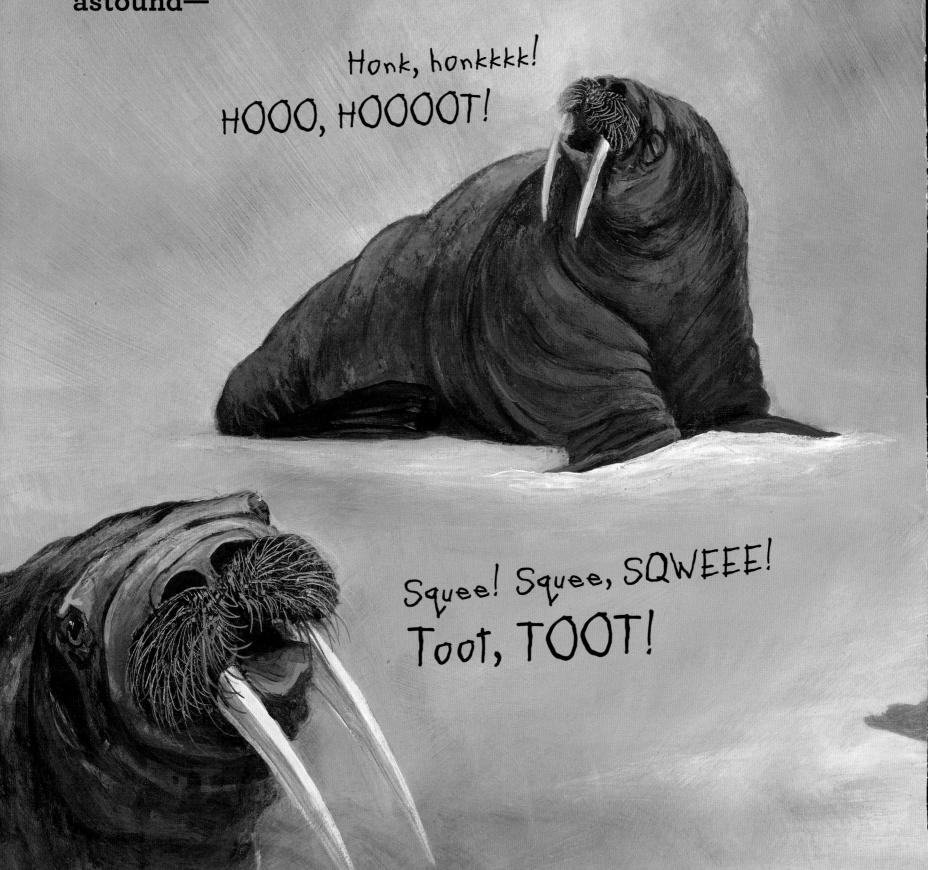

Honk, honkkkk!
HOOO, HOOOOT!

Squee! Squee, SQWEEE!
Toot, TOOT!

Ding, DONG, DONG
Roar! Rrrroar, RROOAARRRR!

Walrus noises
never bore!

Later, babies born in spring
herd with mamas, closely cling.

Far off on another floe,
Walrus tumbles.
Watch him go!

Shimmy-shaking,
big splash making,
ocean quaking.

Walrus,
by and in the sea.
What will his tomorrow be?

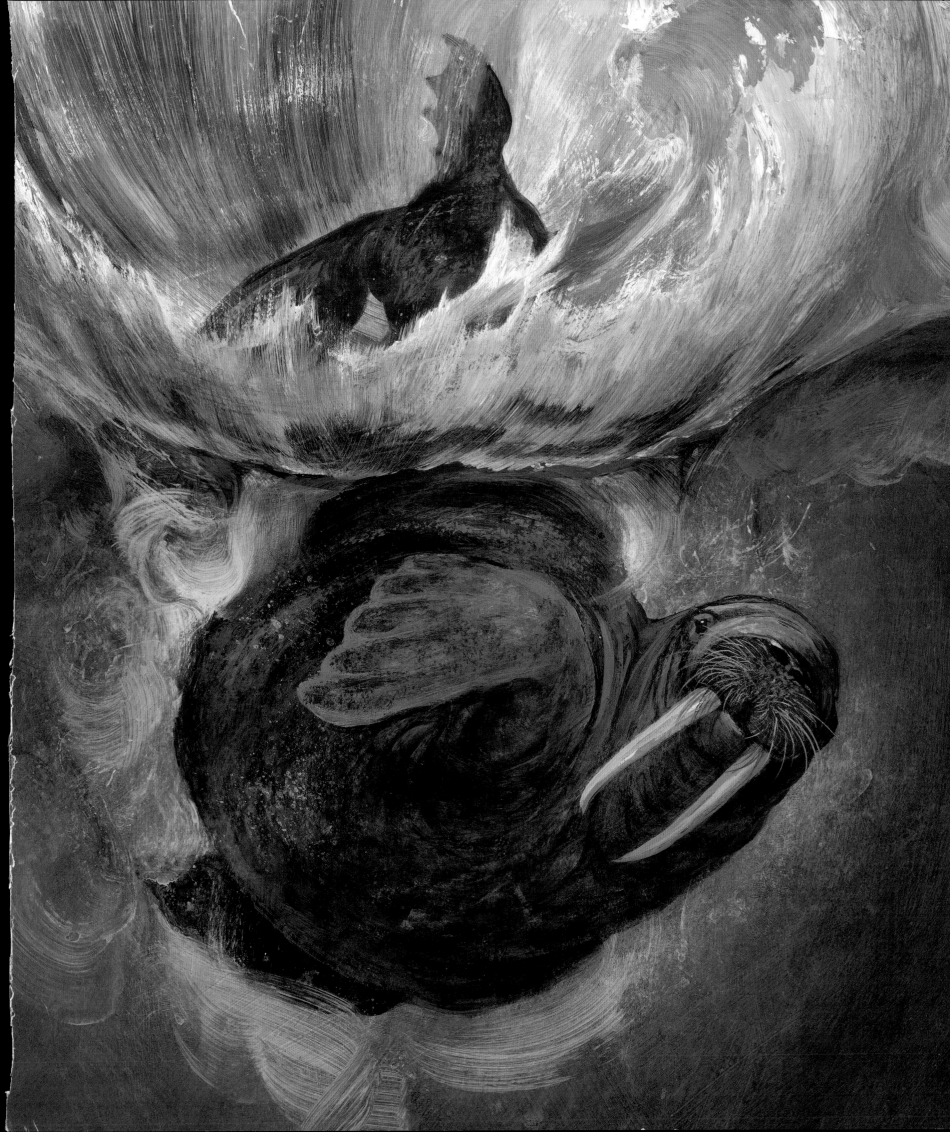

WALRUS FACTS

"On a floe"

A floe is a sheet of ice floating on a body of water. Floes can cover areas many times larger than a soccer field. Hundreds of walruses herd together to rest, sleep, and socialize.

"Twirling, whirling, flippers swirling"

A walrus swims by wiggling its whole body and stroking with its back flippers. It steers with its front flippers.

"warm . . . solid, massive like a boat"

Some walruses weigh more than 3,500 pounds (1,500 kilograms). That's as heavy as a car!

The fat layer under the skin can be almost 6 inches (15 centimeters) thick. This blubber keeps a walrus warm and stores energy.

"In icy waters . . . bivalves thrive"

A walrus eats bivalves such as clams and mussels. These shellfish have two parts (valves) held together by a hinge. A walrus may eat more than 4,000 clams during one feeding frenzy! Walruses also eat shrimp, crabs, tube worms, and other soft-bodied sea animals.

"Digging, wiggling. . . . Seafloor stewing"

Like a bristled brush, a walrus's snout sweeps along the ocean floor. Its whiskers are sense organs that feel for clams and other food.

A walrus also flaps its front flippers and squirts water jets from its mouth to uncover buried shellfish.

"Lips on shells . . . leaving shucks"

A walrus sucks out clam meat by a strong pulling action of its tongue. Chew before swallowing? Not a walrus! It gulps its prey whole and leaves the shucks (shells) behind.

"Belly full. . . . surprise! Away!"

Scientists report that walruses seem to play with birds floating in open seas. Like a jack-in-the-box, a swimming walrus pops up from below and scares a bird away.

"Gleaming tusks . . . up and out"

Both males and females grow tusks that are actually two very long upper teeth. The tusks of adult males may grow more than 3 feet (1 meter) long. Now, that's an overbite! Tusks help a walrus lift and drag its heavy body out of the water. They are also used to chip at ice to make diving holes from above and breathing holes from below.

"Waddle. Walk. . . . Flippers flap"

A walrus swivels its back flippers to face them forward for walking. Thick, rough skin on these flippers helps grip land or ice.

"*Now* where's Walrus? . . . nudge and nuzzle"

Walruses crowd alongside and on top of one another, looking like huge sacks of potatoes. Pairs of gleaming ivory tusks poke out every which way. Males and females herd together during winter mating season. They form separate groups at other times of the year, with females caring for the young.

"Walrus fight . . . tusks a-bashing"

Males spar to decide who's in charge. They roar, wave, and jab their tusks. This bickering happens more often during mating times.

"What's the ruckus?"

Walruses make many sounds for many reasons, such as warning of danger, calling a calf, keeping order, attracting mates, or claiming resting spots. Walruses may chatter, cry, snort, screech, growl, burp, and bellow. Like a crazy crowd at a carnival, a walrus herd is really, really noisy!

"Walrus noises never bore!"

A male walrus is called a bull. He makes loud and varied calls from his small territory in the water. He warns other males to stay out and invites females to come in. Air sacs in a bull's throat help him make deep bell-ringing sounds while underwater. As he surfaces, he keeps up his mating call with whistles and clacks.

"Later, babies . . . closely cling"

A female walrus is called a cow. She gives birth to one calf about every two to three years. Calves stay with mothers for over two years. Like a human hugging a baby, a cow may clutch its calf to its chest and dive into the water to escape danger.

"Shimmy-shaking. . . . What will his tomorrow be?"

Global warming, hunting, and poaching for ivory tusks are threats to all walruses. Healthy habitats and protective laws will help keep these social animals living by and in our arctic waters.

To Anne and Alli
JL

For my mom, dad, and family—my rocks.
For the amazing Candlewick team—remote, and getting it done with excellence.
For Chris Paul, who loves walruses, and whose voice is always present when my
brushes are dripping with paint and my fingers are covered with charcoal.
Walrus-size appreciation for you all!
TBE

Text copyright © 2021 by Janet Lawler
Illustrations copyright © 2021 by Timothy Basil Ering

First edition 2021

Library of Congress Catalog Card Number pending
ISBN 978-1-5362-0755-2

21 22 23 24 25 26 CCP 10 9 8 7 6 5 4 3 2 1

Printed in Shenzhen, Guangdong, China

This book was typeset in Archer.
The illustrations were done in charcoal and acrylic paint on paper.

Candlewick Press
99 Dover Street
Somerville, Massachusetts 02144

www.candlewick.com